REBEL GIRLS

Little Library

10 Women who Create Art

This is a work of creative nonfiction. It is a collection of heartwarming and thought-provoking stories inspired by the lives and adventures of influential women. It is not an encyclopedic account of the events and accomplishments of their lives.

www.rebelgirls.com

Rebel Girls, Inc.
421 Elm Ave.
Larkspur, CA 94939

Text by Dinah Dunn
Art direction by Giulia Flamini
Graphic design by Kristen Brittain
Graphic design and additional illustrations: Alessandro Raimondo
Portrait illustrations: 4: Cherise Harris, 8: Monica Ahanonu,
12: Helena Morais Soares, 16: Angela Hire, 20: Elena De Santi,
24: Giulia Flamini, 28: Sami Bayly, 32: Tiffany Baker,
36: Cristina Portoland, 40: Story Hemi-Morehouse

Printed in China, 2023
10 9 8 7 6 5 4 3 2 1
ISBN: 979-8-88964-072-1

FSC
www.fsc.org
MIX
Paper | Supporting responsible forestry
FSC™ C018179

CONTENTS

Augusta Savage

Sculptor

February 29, 1892–March 26, 1962 | USA

Once, in Florida, there was a girl named Augusta. She had 13 brothers and sisters but not one toy. She loved digging her hands into the red clay in her backyard. Instead of making mud pies, she'd mold the clay into ducks and other animals. But her parents didn't want her to be an artist.

Augusta didn't give up. When she was almost 30 years old, she moved to Harlem in New York City. She went to art school and studied sculpture.

Augusta won a prize to go to an art school in Paris. But when the school found out she was Black, they took back the prize. Augusta spoke out about it, so it wouldn't happen to other Black artists.

Augusta continued to make amazing sculptures. She created one of her nephew, called *Gamin*. It won her a prize—another trip to study art in Paris! Six years after she had been turned away, she could finally make the trip. Augusta was thrilled. When she returned to the United States, she turned her studio in Harlem into a free school for artists.

In 1939, Augusta was the only Black artist asked to created work for the World's Fair in Queens, New York. The goal of the Fair was to show what the United States would be like in the future. Augusta made a 16-foot-tall sculpture. It showed 12 singing Black children standing on the hand of God. They looked like

they were the strings of a harp, so it was called *The Harp*. It was seen by the more than 40 million people who visited.

After the Fair, Augusta didn't have the money to move the sculpture or remake it. Sadly, it was destroyed. But her other artwork, including *Gamin*, can still be found in museums today.

Edmonia Lewis

Sculptor

Circa 1844–September 17, 1907 | USA and Italy

Once upon a time, there was a little girl called Wildfire. Her father, who was Black, and her mother, who was Ojibwe, both died when she was young. Wildfire grew up in her mother's tribe. She spent a lot of time swimming, fishing, and making crafts.

When Wildfire was a young woman, she no longer wanted to be called by her Ojibwe name. When she went to college in 1859, she used her given name, Mary Edmonia Lewis—or just Edmonia, for short.

At college, she enjoyed art. But it was hard to be one of the only Black women at the school. Some students didn't like her. Two students even said she had poisoned them! *It isn't true!* Edmonia said. Still, she had to leave the college.

Around 1863, Edmonia moved to Boston to become a sculptor. In those days, people thought sculpting was only for men. She was tired of not being thought of as an artist because of her race and because she was a woman.

A few years later, Edmonia moved to Rome. There she met a group of women sculptors. She started to work in marble. Other sculptors got help from men to carve the hard stone. But not Edmonia! She did it all herself.

In 1876, she created a sculpture of the death of the Egyptian queen Cleopatra. It took her four years to complete. She brought it to America, where it was sold. The owner didn't take care of it and over time it was covered in paint. But luckily, it was found and cleaned. It can now be seen at the Smithsonian American Art Museum.

SCAN TO HEAR MORE!

Frida Kahlo

Painter

July 6, 1907–July 13, 1954 | Mexico

Once upon a time, in a bright-blue house near Mexico City, there lived a small girl called Frida. She would grow up to be a famous painter. But she almost didn't grow up at all.

When Frida was six years old, she nearly died from polio. The disease left her with a limp when she walked. But that didn't stop her from playing, swimming, and wrestling just like all the other kids.

Then, when she was 18, she was in a terrible bus accident. She almost died again. She had to spend months in bed while her broken bones healed. Her mother figured out a way for her to paint while lying down. Soon, Frida painted all the time.

Frida was often alone as she healed. Many of her paintings were self-portraits. "I am the person I know best," she said. She often showed her pain, love, and feelings in her paintings.

As soon as she was able to walk again, she went to see Mexico's most famous artist, Diego Rivera. *Are my paintings any good?* she asked him.

Her paintings were amazing: bright and beautiful. He fell in love with them—and he fell in love with

Frida. Diego and Frida got married. He was a big man in a large floppy hat. She looked tiny beside him. People called them "the elephant and the dove."

Frida's art became popular. She painted when she could, but she was still in a lot of pain. Her health got worse and she died when she was 47. But her bright-blue house remains just as she left it, full of color and joy and flowers.

SCAN TO HEAR MORE!

Fashion Designer

Born October 23, 1996 | Guatemala

For as long as she could remember, Isabella dreamed of being a fashion designer, just like her grandma. She spent hours looking at fashion magazines. She created dolls as big as she was so she could design dresses for them.

When Isabella grew up, she wanted to go to fashion school. But there was a problem. Isabella had Down syndrome, which made learning a little more difficult for her. The fashion university didn't think she could keep up. Isabella refused to give up. *I know I can be an amazing fashion designer*, she thought.

Isabella kept learning. She went to dressmaking school. She learned how to sew and pin fabrics. She used bold colors and patterns from her home country of Guatemala.

Isabella's hard work paid off. In 2015, she was asked to show her designs at a museum. All of the clothes in the show quickly sold out. Isabella's career had truly begun.

The following year, she showed more designs at London Fashion Week. She was also the first designer with Down syndrome in the International Fashion Showcase.

The university might not have believed in Isabella, but Isabella believed in herself. She now helps support other people with Down syndrome, who are often shaped

differently. It was difficult for Isabella to find clothes growing up. "My mother always had to fix the clothes she bought for me," said Isabella. "So I decided to design clothes that fit people with Down syndrome."

She also reuses old fabric in her designs. Artists in Guatemala help create her tassels, beads, and fringes. All of her embroidery is made by people with disabilities. "I encourage everyone to follow their dreams and to let their minds fly!" Isabella says.

SCAN TO HEAR MORE!

Marjane Satrapi

Graphic Novelist

Born November 22, 1969 | Iran and France

Once there was a girl who used her art to stand up to an unfair government. When Marjane was young, big changes happened in Iran. It started with a revolution that caused a change in the government. At first, some people thought the revolution might be a good thing. People cheered in the streets the day it happened.

After the revolution, though, the new leaders of Iran had a lot of rules. Each time the government created a new rule, Marjane would fight it. She stood up for what she believed in. When the government said all women must wear veils, Marjane let her hair show. When it said no sneakers and jeans, she wore them anyway. When some music was banned, she found a way to listen to it. And when her teachers spoke of Iran's leaders, she asked brave questions.

Marjane's parents were proud of their daughter, but they were scared too. She could go to jail! To keep her safe, they sent her to boarding school in Austria. After high school, Marjane moved to France to study art. She had always loved comics, so she created some of her own.

Using simple black-and-white drawings, she told the story of her childhood in Iran. She wrote about how she wanted to change her world. And most of all, she learned to follow a rule she learned from her grandma: always be true to yourself.

Her graphic novel, *Persepolis*, was published. It became a bestseller all over the world. Later, Marjane helped turn the book into a movie. Marjane lives in France. But she continues to use art to tell stories about her home country.

Maud Stevens Wagner

Tattoo Artist

February 1877–January 30, 1961 | USA

Maud left her small town in Kansas and joined the circus. She learned to fly through the air on a trapeze. She could also bend and twist her body into tiny spaces. People would pay to see her amazing feats every night.

During the 1904 World's Fair, she met an interesting man named Gus Wagner. His body was covered with hundreds of tattoos he had collected all over the world. He had monkeys, butterflies, lions, horses, snakes, trees, women—anything you can think of! *I am a walking, talking work of art!* he used to say.

Maud loved his tattoos! She said she would go out with him . . . if he gave her a tattoo. Gus agreed. What began with one became dozens of tattoos. Soon Maud's body was completely covered, just like Gus's. But if she wore long sleeves and skirts, no one could tell.

Maud was a quick learner. She began working as a tattooist for other circus performers. She was the first known female tattoo artist in the United States.

At the time, tattoos were unusual. People would go to the circus to see performers with skin covered in ink. Maud also started tattooing people in the audience. They often asked for images of their pets.

Maud and Gus loved working together. Plus, they made a lot of money. They eventually got married and had a daughter, Lotteva. Maud made Gus promise not to tattoo their daughter. Lotteva never got a tattoo, but her mother inspired her. She started giving tattoos when she was only nine years old!

Sami Bayly

Author and Illustrator

Born February 13, 1996 | Australia

Once there was a girl who saw the beauty in every animal. Sami and her family lived in a house full of pets—dogs, guinea pigs, rabbits, fish, birds, ponies, cows, and donkeys! Young Sami and her artist mom painted them all.

While Sami's mom created huge portraits, Sami sometimes had trouble drawing her furry friends. But she kept trying. Sami would look up at walls filled with her mother's paintings and think, *Mine will look like that one day too*. She kept drawing and painting. Then she studied art in college.

Sami loved birds, but she knew other people didn't. For example, many Australians hated the

Australian white ibis. These birds steal crusts of bread, french fries, and other food out of garbage cans. She decided to use her years of practice to show people how lovely the bird could be.

Sami took out her paints, brushes, and a large sheet of paper. She painted carefully, layering color to show the ibis's dark, curved beak and white feathers. Then she posted the painting on social media.

Sami had hoped a few people would fall in love with the ibis. But her painting went viral! Sami soon found herself writing and illustrating a book for kids. *The Illustrated Encyclopaedia of Ugly Animals* has more than 60 odd creatures in it. One of Sami's favorites is the Surinam toad, which is as flat as a pancake. Its babies are born out of the mother toad's back.

Readers can't get enough of her portraits of animals. Sami's paintings don't look like her mom's. Her art style is all her own. And it's making people around the world look at "ugly" animals in a whole new way.

Sasha Huber

Artist

Born April 24, 1975 | Switzerland and Finland

How far would you go for something you believed in? How about to the top of a tall mountain in Switzerland? That's what the artist Sasha Huber did!

One day, Sasha's sister gave her a book about slavery in Switzerland. In it, she read that a nearby mountain top was named after the 19th-century scientist Louis Agassiz. He was well known for his work in natural history. But he was also known for his belief that Black people were not as human as white people.

To try to prove this idea, Louis studied and photographed enslaved people. Sasha saw his famous photos of two enslaved people, Renty and his daughter, Delia, in a book. She thought, *Louis shouldn't have a mountain named after him!* So she decided to use her art to make a difference, like her family had done.

Sasha's grandfather, who lived in Haiti, was an amazing artist. She didn't visit when she was young because the country was dangerous. However, after she went to art school, she used the history of her grandfather's country in her work.

Sasha and the author of the slavery book came up with a plan. They would rename the mountain after Renty! That way people all over the world would learn about him.

Sasha wrote Renty's story on a metal sign, got in a helicopter, and flew to the mountaintop. She walked

shows them with their eyes closed against the world.

Shamsia knows her art won't change Afghanistan on its own. She says, "Art can only change people's minds, and then people's minds can change the society. That is what I hope for."

SCAN TO HEAR MORE!

Te Manaia Jennings

Painter and Mental Health Advocate

Born January 3, 2000 | New Zealand

Te Manaia spent a lot of time in the hospital. Her spine was curved, so she had to get many surgeries. Her body was covered in scars. She was sad and worried. *Will I ever get better?* she thought.

Te Manaia needed a way to deal with all of her big feelings. Drawing and painting helped. Art was a way for her to say how she felt without using words.

She painted faces in colors that showed their moods. Some of the people in her paintings were crying, others were smiling. Slowly, Te Manaia started to feel different about art and herself.

Painting also became a way for her to explore her feelings about being

Māori. The Māori are an Indigenous people in New Zealand. Growing up there, Te Manaia saw that Māori people were not treated the same as white people. It made them feel bad about their race. She wanted to change that with her art. She adds a lot of Māori designs and history to her paintings.

"I saw an opportunity to be a voice for young people," Te Manaia said. She wants them to understand: "It's OK to be sad. It's OK to not always feel good. Everyone has bad days."

Art has not only helped Te Manaia cope with her feelings. It has also changed the way she thinks about her body. "I like my scars now, and I like showing them off because it shows strength," she says. "It shows my story."

About Rebel Girls

Rebel Girls is a global, multi-platform empowerment brand dedicated to helping raise the most inspired and confident generation of girls through content, experiences, products, and community. Originating from an international best-selling children's book, Rebel Girls amplifies stories of real-life women throughout history, geography, and field of excellence. With a growing community of nearly 20 million self-identified Rebel Girls spanning more than 100 countries, the brand engages with Generation Alpha through its book series, award-winning podcast, events, and merchandise. With the 2021 launch of the Rebel Girls app, the company has created a flagship destination for girls to explore a wondrous world filled with inspiring true stories of extraordinary women.

As a B Corp, we're part of a global community of businesses that meet high standards of social and environmental impact.

Join the Rebel Girls community:

Facebook: facebook.com/rebelgirls
Instagram: @rebelgirls
Twitter: @rebelgirlsbook
TikTok: @rebelgirlsbook
Web: rebelgirls.com
Podcast: rebelgirls.com/podcast
App: rebelgirls.com/audio

If you liked this book, please take a moment to review it wherever you prefer!